Guru Nanak

SRI JAPJI SAHIB
*English translation from
the original Gurmukhi*

ਜਪੁਜੀ ਸਾਹਿਬ

Guru Nanak

"*He who lowers his mind to the dust of all men's feet, Sees the Name of God enshrined in every heart.*"

--Guru Arjan

ਜਪੁਜੀ ਸਾਹਿਬ

Guru Nanak

SRI JAPJI SAHIB
English translation from the original Gurmukhi

Format Design by
David Christopher Lane

Mt. San Antonio College
Walnut, California

ਜਪੁਜੀ ਸਾਹਿਬ

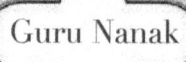

Guru Nanak

SRI JAPJI SAHIB

Format Copyright © 2018
by MSAC Philosophy Group

Trade paperback | Second Edition

ISBN: 978-1-56543-797-5

MSAC *Philosophy Group* was founded in 1990 and is designed to provide a wide range of materials (from books to magazines to films to audio presentations to interactive texts) on such subjects as evolutionary biology, quantum theory, neuroscience, and critical studies in religion and philosophy. All books are sold on a not for profit basis. Free PDF versions are made available whenever possible. In addition, there is a growing collection of audio books specifically created for students at Mt. San Antonio College and the community at large. A large series of original movies have also been produced which touch on such topics as artificial intelligence, eliminative materialism, consciousness, and skepticism.

ਜਪੁਜੀ ਸਾਹਿਬ

INTRODUCTION

Although I am not a Sikh, I have long been deeply impressed by the teachings of Guru Nanak and his nine successors. Indeed, I believe that the *Sri Guru Granth Sahib*, the sacred writings of Sikhism, is unique amongst the world's religions. Not only does it contain the hymns of six of the Sikh gurus, but also of the Sant poets Kabir, Ravidas, and Namdev. The universal and eclectic nature of the *Sri Guru Granth Sahib* is perhaps best epitomized by its inclusion of poems by the revered Muslim mystic, Sheikh Farid.

When I was but eighteen years old, I chanced upon Gopal Singh's English translation of the *Sri Guru Granth Sahib* at the now defunct bookstore, Bodhi Tree, in West Hollywood. Beautifully bound in a special four-volume set, I immediately wanted to buy it but the price was prohibitive for me at that time. It was 80 dollars. Having already read excerpts from Guru Nanak's beautiful teachings, I was determined to read the entire holy book. So I saved money from my job as a "box boy" at the local market and within a couple of weeks bought the entire set. Nearly forty-five years later I still own this treasured possession.

ਜਪੁਜੀ ਸਾਹਿਬ

The *Sri Japji Sahib* was composed by Guru Nanak and is the opening prayer of the *Sri Guru Granth Sahib.* It is widely regarded as containing the heart of Sikh teachings.

Sri Japji Sahib was first published in Gurmukhi in 1604. There are now several English translations of the text, but nothing can compare to actually listening to it sung aloud when visiting the exquisite Golden Temple of the Sikhs in Amritsar, Punjab, India.

I have visited the Golden Temple several times, but my most memorable experience was in

March 21st of 2017 when my family and I got the privilege of visiting the sacred center at night. In the essay, "Devotional Thickness: The Sacredness of Human Longing," specially written for *Integral World* in Europe, I explain what transpired: I didn't expect to be overwhelmed with emotion and I certainly didn't expect to be transformed by the experience. But there I was witnessing something quite astonishing, and right in the midst of it a long forgotten book title by C.S. Lewis came to the forefront of my mind-- *Surprised by Joy*. The atmosphere was electric, but what struck me most forcefully was the

V

unconditional love that permeated the surroundings. It was on the night of March 21, 2017, and I wanted to see the holiest of Sikh Gurdwaras, the Golden Temple. My family and I had just arrived in Amritsar in the Punjab just a few hours prior on Vistara Airlines from Delhi. I was in India conducting research for a new project for Oxford University Press and only had 12 or so hours before having to travel to Beas. Although I had first visited the Golden Temple in the summer of 1978 (which, coincidentally was also connected with a research project on the same subject), I had never seen it at night.

ਜਪੁਜੀ ਸਾਹਿਬ

vi

I knew that the surrounding area had been dramatically renovated and that the Golden Temple had become increasingly popular as a tourist destination, but what I hadn't realized was how crowded it had become at almost all hours of the day. There are several factors that make the *Sri Harmandir Sahib* (literally, "Abode of God") unique. One immediately notices, for instance, that there are no security checkpoints for entering into the complex. No visible metal detectors, no frisking by armed guards, no restrictions of any kind on who may or may not enter the sacred grounds.

ਜਪੁਜੀ ਸਾਹਿਬ

All that is required is to wear proper attire, going barefoot so as to cleanse one's feet before entering, and wearing a head covering. Sikhism was founded by Guru Nanak, who was born in the latter part of the 15th century and established a lineage of nine succeeding human gurus (from Guru Angad to Guru Gobind Singh). It was the tenth guru in the 18th century who proclaimed that the holy writings of six of the Sikh gurus along with selected writings from such Sants as Kabir, Namdev, and the Sufi mystic, Sheikh Farid, would serve as the "final and eternal living guru" for all followers of the Sikh religion.

Written in Gurmukhi script, the *Sri Guru Granth Sahib* is held in the highest respect by Sikhs worldwide since it contains the essence of their spiritual philosophy. The book is housed in the innermost sanctum of the Golden Temple and is recited daily and is treated with the utmost care. Our driver, with the very apt and accurate name of "Happy", wanted my family and I to have a glimpse of the inner sanctum of the *Sri Harmandir Sahib*, even though it was just after 10 p.m. at night when a palanquin (known as the *Palki Sahib*) carries the sacred holy book of the Sikhs, the *Sri Guru Granth Sahib* to the *Akal*

ਜਪੁਜੀ ਸਾਹਿਬ

Takhat Sahib. At this time, visitors (especially foreigners) are discouraged from entering the temple since devotees clean the *Sri Harmandir Sahib* for an hour or so. Fortunately, however, due to "Happy's" persistence we were allowed to witness the diligent work of these Sikh sevadars as they sang in the most intense and enchanting way the *Gurbani Kirtan*. I cannot even begin to describe how completely engaged and sincere the many *sevadars* were in doing the cleaning. It wasn't perfunctory in the least, but rather seen as a great honor to be able to do such work.

ਜਪੁਜੀ ਸਾਹਿਬ

X

And one could palpably feel the energy, the excitement, and the yearning underlying the devotional singing. It was a surreal scene, the likes of which I will never forget. Although I was raised as a Roman Catholic, it was impossible not to be transfixed by the magnificence of the Golden Temple, but even more by the earnest love and devotion I personally saw among the vast throng who felt blessed by being able to glimpse their beloved guru. Coming home, late that night, I realized anew that what makes something sacred or numinous is the earnest desire of humans for that which transcends them.

ਜਪੁਜੀ ਸਾਹਿਬ

While I am sure there is a better description for what I witnessed, somehow the phrase "Devotional Thickness" rung true. It is a human product and as such can illuminate and shine forth at anytime, anywhere, and at any place. It is not restricted to any particular ism and because of this, it can manifest unexpectedly. Of course, some places and some gatherings tend to bring out the very best in us and because of such, they become "sacred". The sanctity is not necessarily geographical (though that too does play a part), but rather part and parcel of our biological (and biographical) make-up.

xii

Bring the deepest yearning in a human being to the forefront and you have the very best of spirituality, even if it is in a conference room filled with agnostics and atheists. What transforms is the human heart and what I saw at the Golden Temple was both simple and profound: a wide diversity of people bringing their "best" selves and their "deepest" aspirations. It makes perfect sense, regardless of one's religious affiliation (or lack thereof) to want to visit such communal centers of worship. As we all know, the world has far too many areas where humans bring their worst selves and act accordingly.

ਜਪੁਜੀ ਸਾਹਿਬ

xiii

Even though there is much to criticize about religion, it is vitally important to remember that at certain times and in certain places unbounded human longing can be allowed to flourish and it is then and there that we can get a glimpse of the transcendent. This unique human quality, which in German is called *Sehnsucht* ("intensely missing"), can manifest wherever and whenever we acknowledge the mystery that both precedes and transcends us— whether it is a gathering of astronomers pondering the deepest reaches of the Milky Way or devoted Sikhs honoring the wisdom of their Gurus and their teachings.

ਜਪੁਜੀ ਸਾਹਿਬ

xiv

The Golden Temple
Amritsar, Punjab, India

Sri Harmandir Sahib

ਸ੍ਰੀ ਹਰਮਿੰਦਰ ਸਾਹਿਬ

ਜਪੁਜੀ ਸਾਹਿਬ

1

One Universal Creator God.

The Name Is Truth. Creative Being Personified. No Fear. No Hatred.

Image Of The Undying, Beyond Birth, Self-Existent. By Guru's Grace ~

ਜਪੁਜੀ ਸਾਹਿਬ

2

Chant And Meditate:

True In The Primal Beginning.

True Throughout The Ages.

True Here And Now.

O Nanak, Forever And Ever True.

ਜਪੁਜੀ ਸਾਹਿਬ

3

By thinking, He cannot be reduced to thought, even by thinking hundreds of thousands of times.
By remaining silent, inner silence is not obtained, even by remaining lovingly absorbed deep within.

ਜਪੁਜੀ ਸਾਹਿਬ

4

The hunger of the hungry is not appeased, even by piling up loads of worldly goods. Hundreds of thousands of clever tricks, but not even one of them will go along with you in the end.

ਜਪੁਜੀ ਸਾਹਿਬ

5

So how can you become truthful? And how can the veil of illusion be torn away? O Nanak, it is written that you shall obey the Hukam of His Command, and walk in the Way of His Will.

ਜਪੁਜੀ ਸਾਹਿਬ

6

By His Command, bodies are created; His Command cannot be described.
By His Command, souls come into being; by His Command, glory and greatness are obtained.
By His Command, some are high and some are low; by His Written Command, pain and pleasure are obtained.

7

Some, by His Command, are blessed and forgiven; others, by His Command, wander aimlessly forever. Everyone is subject to His Command; no one is beyond His Command. O Nanak, one who understands His Command, does not speak in ego.

ਜਪੁਜੀ ਸਾਹਿਬ

8

Some sing of His
Power-who has that
Power?

Some sing of His Gifts,
and know His Sign and
Insignia.

Some sing of His
Glorious Virtues,
Greatness and Beauty.

ਜਪੁਜੀ ਸਾਹਿਬ

9

Some sing of knowledge obtained of Him, through difficult philosophical studies.

Some sing that He fashions the body, and then again reduces it to dust.

Some sing that He takes life away, and then again restores it.

ਜਪੁਜੀ ਸਾਹਿਬ

10

Some sing that He
seems so very far away.

Some sing that He
watches over us, face to
face, ever-present.

ਜਪੁਜੀ ਸਾਹਿਬ

There is no shortage of those who preach and teach.

Millions upon millions offer millions of sermons and stories.

The Great Giver keeps on giving, while those who receive grow weary of receiving.

12

Throughout the ages, consumers consume.

The Commander, by His Command, leads us to walk on the Path.

O Nanak, He blossoms forth, Carefree and Untroubled.

ਜਪੁਜੀ ਸਾਹਿਬ

13

True is the Master,
True is His Name-speak
it with infinite love.

People beg and pray,
"Give to us, give to us",
and the Great Giver
gives His Gifts.

So what offering can we
place before Him, by
which we might see the
Darbaar of His Court?

ਜਪੁਜੀ ਸਾਹਿਬ

14

What words can we speak to evoke His Love?

In the *Amrit Vaylaa*, the ambrosial hours before dawn, chant the True Name, and contemplate His Glorious Greatness.

ਜਪੁਜੀ ਸਾਹਿਬ

15

By the karma of past actions, the robe of this physical body is obtained. By His Grace, the Gate of Liberation is found.

O Nanak, know this well: the True One Himself is All.

ਜਪੁਜੀ ਸਾਹਿਬ

16

He cannot be established, He cannot be created.

He Himself is Immaculate and Pure.

Those who serve Him are honored.

ਜਪੁਜੀ ਸਾਹਿਬ

O Nanak, sing of the Lord, the Treasure of Excellence.

Sing, and listen, and let your mind be filled with love.

Your pain shall be sent far away, and peace shall come to your home.

18

The Guru's Word is the Sound-current of the Naad; the Guru's Word is the Wisdom of the Vedas; the Guru's Word is all-pervading.

The Guru is Shiva, the Guru is Vishnu and Brahma; the Guru is Paarvati and Lakhshmi.

ਜਪੁਜੀ ਸਾਹਿਬ

19

Even knowing God, I cannot describe Him; He cannot be described in words.

The Guru has given me this one understanding: there is only the One, the Giver of all souls. May I never forget Him!

ਜਪੁਜੀ ਸਾਹਿਬ

20

If I am pleasing to Him, then that is my pilgrimage and cleansing bath. Without pleasing Him, what good are ritual cleansings?

I gaze upon all the created beings: without the karma of good actions, what are they given to receive?

ਜਪੁਜੀ ਸਾਹਿਬ

21

Within the mind are gems, jewels and rubies, if you listen to the Guru's Teachings, even once.

The Guru has given me this one understanding: there is only the One, the Giver of all souls. May I never forget Him!

ਜਪੁਜੀ ਸਾਹਿਬ

22

Even if you could live throughout the four ages, or even ten times more, and even if you were known throughout the nine continents and followed by all, with a good name and reputation, with praise and fame throughout the world-still, if the Lord does not bless you with His Glance of Grace, then who cares?

ਜਪੁਜੀ ਸਾਹਿਬ

What is the use?

Among worms, you would be considered a lowly worm, and even contemptible sinners would hold you in contempt.

O Nanak, God blesses the unworthy with virtue, and bestows virtue on the virtuous.

ਜਪੁਜੀ ਸਾਹਿਬ

No one can even imagine anyone who can bestow virtue upon Him.

Listening-the Siddhas, the spiritual teachers, the heroic warriors, the yogic masters.

Listening-the earth, its support and the Akaashic ethers.

25

Listening-the oceans,
the lands of the world
and the nether regions
of the underworld.

Listening-Death cannot
even touch you.

O Nanak, the devotees
are forever in bliss.

26

Listening--pain and sin are erased.

Listening--Shiva, Brahma and Indra.

Listening--even foul-mouthed people praise Him.

ਜਪੁਜੀ ਸਾਹਿਬ

Listening--the technology of Yoga and the secrets of the body.

Listening--the Shaastras, the Simritees and the Vedas.

O Nanak, the devotees are forever in bliss.

Listening--pain and sin are erased.

Listening--truth, contentment and spiritual wisdom.

Listening--take your cleansing bath at the sixty-eight places of pilgrimage.

ਜਪੁਜੀ ਸਾਹਿਬ

29

Listening--reading and reciting, honor is obtained.

Listening--intuitively grasp the essence of meditation.

O Nanak, the devotees are forever in bliss.

ਜਪੁਜੀ ਸਾਹਿਬ

30

Listening--pain and sin
are erased.

Listening--dive deep
into the ocean of virtue.

Listening--the Shaykhs,
religious scholars,
spiritual teachers and
emperors.

31

Listening-even the blind
find the Path.

Listening-the
Unreachable comes
within your grasp.

O Nanak, the devotees
are forever in bliss.

32

Listening--pain and sin are erased.

The state of the faithful cannot be described.

One who tries to describe this shall regret the attempt.

ਜਪੁਜੀ ਸਾਹਿਬ

33

No paper, no pen, no scribe can record the state of the faithful.

Such is the Name of the Immaculate Lord.

Only one who has faith comes to know such a state of mind.

ਜਪੁਜੀ ਸਾਹਿਬ

34

The faithful have intuitive awareness and intelligence.

The faithful know about all worlds and realms.

The faithful shall never be struck across the face.

35

The faithful do not have to go with the Messenger of Death.

Such is the Name of the Immaculate Lord.

Only one who has faith comes to know such a state of mind.

ਜਪੁਜੀ ਸਾਹਿਬ

36

The path of the faithful shall never be blocked.

The faithful shall depart with honor and fame.

The faithful do not follow empty religious rituals.

ਜਪੁਜੀ ਸਾਹਿਬ

37

The faithful are firmly bound to the Dharma.

Such is the Name of the Immaculate Lord.

Only one who has faith comes to know such a state of mind.

ਜਪੁਜੀ ਸਾਹਿਬ

38

The faithful find the Door of Liberation.

The faithful uplift and redeem their family and relations.

The faithful are saved, and carried across with the Sikhs of the Guru.

ਜਪੁਜੀ ਸਾਹਿਬ

39

The faithful, O Nanak, do not wander around begging.

Such is the Name of the Immaculate Lord.

Only one who has faith comes to know such a state of mind.

ਜਪੁਜੀ ਸਾਹਿਬ

40

The chosen ones, the self-elect, are accepted and approved.

The chosen ones are honored in the Court of the Lord.

The chosen ones look beautiful in the courts of kings.

ਜਪੁਜੀ ਸਾਹਿਬ

41

The chosen ones meditate single-mindedly on the Guru.

No matter how much anyone tries to explain and describe them, the actions of the Creator cannot be counted.

ਜਪੁਜੀ ਸਾਹਿਬ

The mythical bull is Dharma, the son of compassion; this is what patiently holds the earth in its place.

One who understands this becomes truthful.

What a great load there is on the bull!

43

So many worlds beyond this world-so very many!

What power holds them, and supports their weight?

The names and the colors of the assorted species of beings were all inscribed by the Ever-flowing Pen of God.

ਜਪੁਜੀ ਸਾਹਿਬ

44

Who knows how to write this account?

Just imagine what a huge scroll it would take!

What power! What fascinating beauty!

ਜਪੁਜੀ ਸਾਹਿਬ

45

And what gifts! Who can know their extent?

You created the vast expanse of the Universe with One Word!

Hundreds of thousands of rivers began to flow.

46

How can Your Creative
Potency be described?

I cannot even once be a
sacrifice to You.

Whatever pleases You is
the only good done,
You, Eternal and
Formless One!

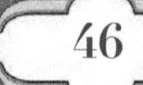

47

Countless meditations,
countless loves.

Countless worship
services, countless
austere disciplines.

Countless scriptures,
and ritual recitations of
the Vedas.

48

Countless Yogis, whose minds remain detached from the world.

Countless devotees contemplate the Wisdom and Virtues of the Lord.

Countless the holy, countless the givers.

49

Countless heroic spiritual warriors, who bear the brunt of the attack in battle (who with their mouths eat steel).

Countless silent sages, vibrating the String of His Love.

How can Your Creative Potency be described?

ਜਪੁਜੀ ਸਾਹਿਬ

50

I cannot even once be a sacrifice to You.

Whatever pleases You is the only good done,

You, Eternal and Formless One.

ਜਪੁਜੀ ਸਾਹਿਬ

51

Countless fools, blinded by ignorance.

Countless thieves and embezzlers.

Countless impose their will by force.

Countless cut-throats and ruthless killers.

52

Countless sinners who keep on sinning.

.

Countless liars, wandering lost in their lies.

Countless wretches, eating filth as their ration.

53

Countless slanderers, carrying the weight of their stupid mistakes on their heads.

Nanak describes the state of the lowly.
I cannot even once be a sacrifice to You.

ਜਪੁਜੀ ਸਾਹਿਬ

54

Whatever pleases You is
the only good done,

.

You, Eternal and
Formless One.

Countless names,
countless places.

ਜਪੁਜੀ ਸਾਹਿਬ

55

Inaccessible, unapproachable, countless celestial realms.

Even to call them countless is to carry the weight on your head.

From the Word, comes the Naam; from the Word, comes Your Praise.

ਜਪੁਜੀ ਸਾਹਿਬ

From the Word, comes spiritual wisdom, singing the Songs of Your Glory.

From the Word, come the written and spoken words and hymns.

From the Word, comes destiny, written on one's forehead.

ਜਪੁਜੀ ਸਾਹਿਬ

57

But the One who wrote these Words of Destiny- no words are written on His Forehead.

As He ordains, so do we receive.

The created universe is the manifestation of Your Name.

Without Your Name, there is no place at all.

ਜਪੁਜੀ ਸਾਹਿਬ

58

How can I describe Your
Creative Power?

I cannot even once be a
sacrifice to You.

Whatever pleases You is
the only good done,
You, Eternal and
Formless One.

59

When the hands and the feet and the body are dirty, water can wash away the dirt.

When the clothes are soiled and stained by urine soap can wash them clean.

ਜਪੁਜੀ ਸਾਹਿਬ

But when the intellect is stained and polluted by sin, it can only be cleansed by the Love of the Name.

ਜਪੁਜੀ ਸਾਹਿਬ

Virtue and vice do not come by mere words; actions repeated, over and over again, are engraved on the soul.

You shall harvest what you plant.

O Nanak, by the Hukam of God's Command, we come and go in reincarnation.

Pilgrimages, austere discipline, compassion and charity--these, by themselves, bring only an iota of merit.

Listening and believing with love and humility in your mind, cleanse yourself with the Name, at the sacred shrine deep within.

ਜਪੁਜੀ ਸਾਹਿਬ

63

All virtues are Yours, Lord, I have none at all.

Without virtue, there is no devotional worship.

I bow to the Lord of the World, to His Word, to Brahma the Creator.

ਜਪੁਜੀ ਸਾਹਿਬ

64

He is Beautiful, True and Eternally Joyful.

What was that time, and what was that moment? What was that day, and what was that date?

What was that season, and what was that month, when the Universe was created?

65

The Pandits, the religious scholars, cannot find that time, even if it is written in the Puraanas.

That time is not known to the Qazis, who study the Koran.

The day and the date are not known to the Yogis, nor is the month or the season.

The Creator who created this creation-only He Himself knows.

How can we speak of Him? How can we praise Him? How can we describe Him? How can we know Him?

O Nanak, everyone speaks of Him, each one wiser than the rest.

Great is the Master,
Great is His Name.
Whatever happens is
according to His Will.

O Nanak, one who
claims to know
everything shall not be
decorated in the world
hereafter.

There are nether worlds
beneath nether worlds,
and hundreds of
thousands of heavenly
worlds above.

The Vedas say that you
can search and search
for them all, until you
grow weary.

ਜਪੁਜੀ ਸਾਹਿਬ

The scriptures say that there are 18,000 worlds, but in reality, there is only One Universe.

If you try to write an account of this, you will surely finish yourself before you finish writing it.

O Nanak, call Him Great! He Himself knows Himself.

The praisers praise the Lord, but they do not obtain intuitive understanding--the streams and rivers flowing into the ocean do not know its vastness.

Even kings and emperors, with mountains of property and oceans of wealth-- these are not even equal to an ant, who does not forget God.

Endless are His Praises, endless are those who speak them.

Endless are His Actions,
endless are His Gifts.

Endless is His Vision,
endless is His Hearing.

His limits cannot be
perceived. What is the
Mystery of His Mind?

The limits of the created universe cannot be perceived.

Its limits here and beyond cannot be perceived.

Many struggle to know His limits, but His limits cannot be found.

No one can know these limits.

The more you say about them, the more there still remains to be said.

Great is the Master, High is His Heavenly Home.

Highest of the High, above all is His Name.

75

Only one as Great and as High as God can know His Lofty and Exalted State.

Only He Himself is that Great. He Himself knows Himself.

O Nanak, by His Glance of Grace, He bestows His Blessings.

ਜਪੁਜੀ ਸਾਹਿਬ

His Blessings are so abundant that there can be no written account of them.

The Great Giver does not hold back anything.

There are so many great, heroic warriors begging at the Door of the Infinite Lord.

ਜਪੁਜੀ ਸਾਹਿਬ

77

So many contemplate and dwell upon Him, that they cannot be counted.

So many waste away to death engaged in corruption.

So many take and take again, and then deny receiving.

ਜਪੁਜੀ ਸਾਹਿਬ

So many foolish consumers keep on consuming.

So many endure distress, deprivation and constant abuse.

Even these are Your Gifts, O Great Giver!

Liberation from bondage comes only by Your Will.

ਜਪੁਜੀ ਸਾਹਿਬ

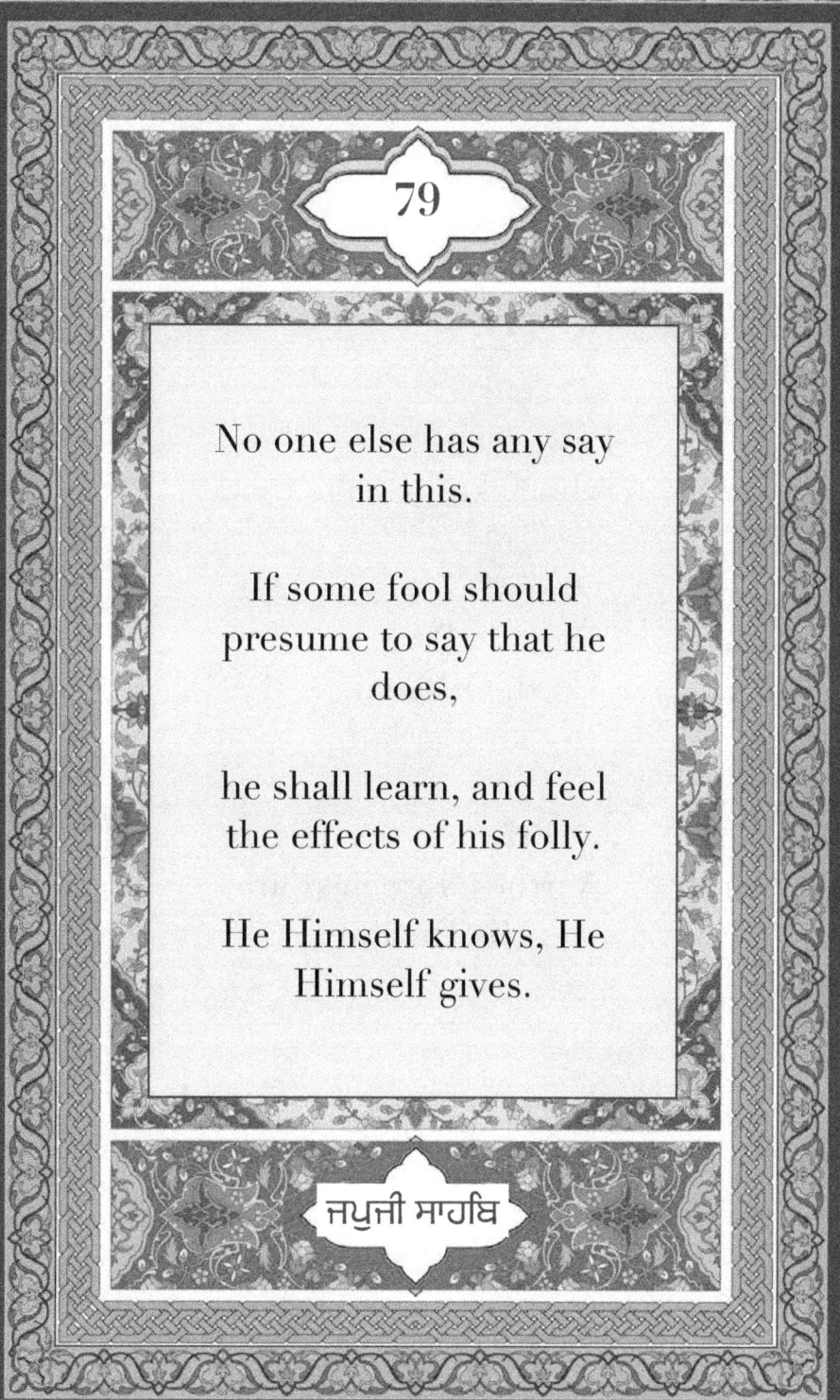

79

No one else has any say in this.

If some fool should presume to say that he does,

he shall learn, and feel the effects of his folly.

He Himself knows, He Himself gives.

ਜਪੁਜੀ ਸਾਹਿਬ

Few, very few are those who acknowledge this.

One who is blessed to sing the Praises of the Lord, O Nanak, is the king of kings.

Priceless are His Virtues, Priceless are His Dealings.

81

Priceless are His Dealers, Priceless are His Treasures.

Priceless are those who come to Him, Priceless are those who buy from Him.

Priceless is Love for Him, Priceless is absorption into Him.

ਜਪੁਜੀ ਸਾਹਿਬ

Priceless is the Divine Law of Dharma, Priceless is the Divine Court of Justice.

Priceless are the scales, priceless are the weights.

Priceless are His Blessings, Priceless is His Banner and Insignia.

ਜਪੁਜੀ ਸਾਹਿਬ

83

Priceless, O Priceless beyond expression!

Speak of Him continually, and remain absorbed in His Love.

The Vedas and the Puraanas speak.

The scholars speak and lecture.

Brahma speaks, Indra speaks.

The Gopis and Krishna speak.

Shiva speaks, the Siddhas speak.

The many created Buddhas speak.

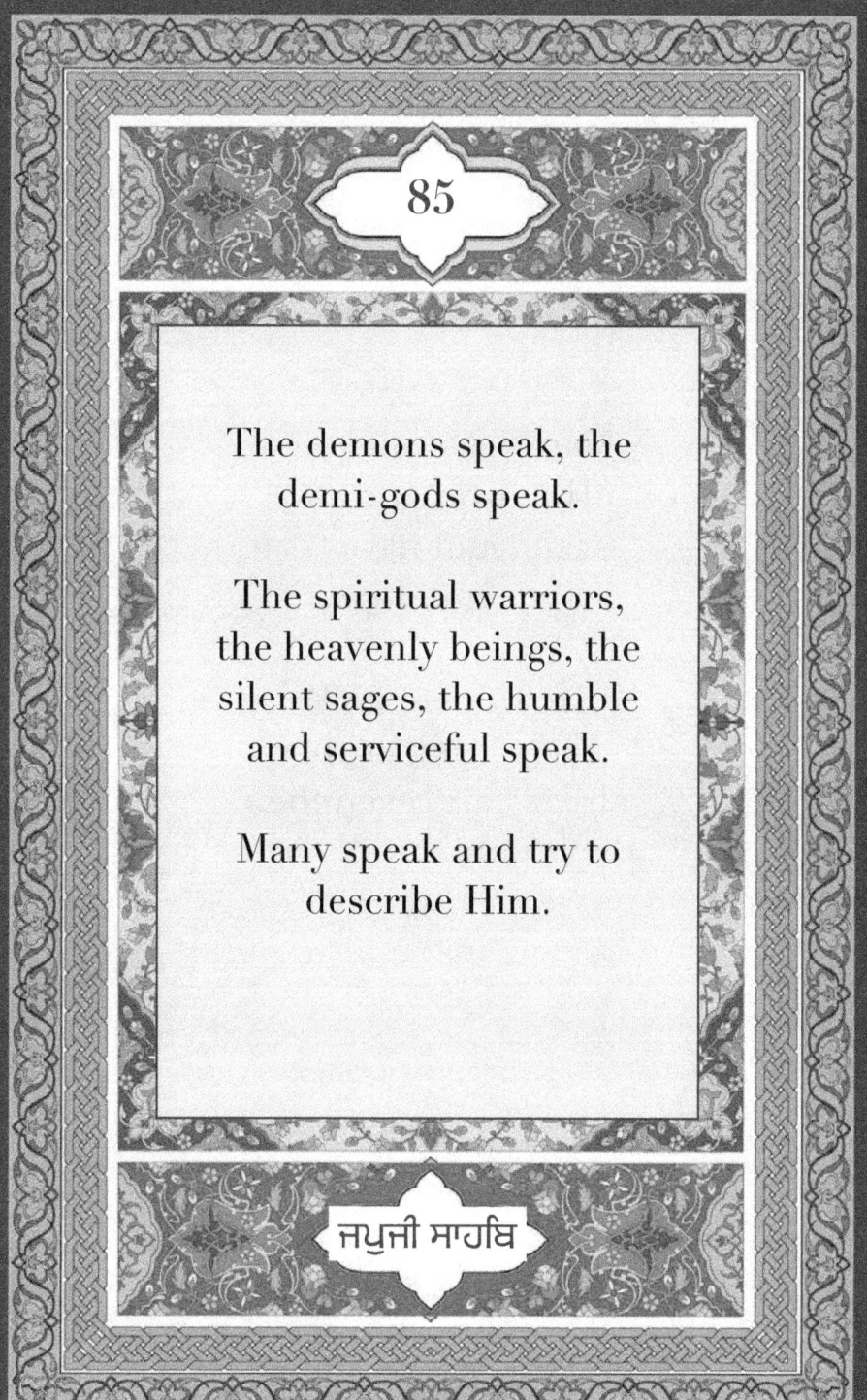

85

The demons speak, the demi-gods speak.

The spiritual warriors, the heavenly beings, the silent sages, the humble and serviceful speak.

Many speak and try to describe Him.

ਜਪੁਜੀ ਸਾਹਿਬ

Many have spoken of Him over and over again, and have then arisen and departed.

If He were to create as many again as there already are, even then, they could not describe Him.

ਜਪੁਜੀ ਸਾਹਿਬ

87

He is as Great as He wishes to be.

O Nanak, the True Lord knows.

If anyone presumes to describe God, he shall be known as the greatest fool of fools!

ਜਪੁਜੀ ਸਾਹਿਬ

Where is that Gate, and where is that Dwelling, in which You sit and take care of all?

The Sound-current of the Naad vibrates there, and countless musicians play on all sorts of instruments there.

89

So many Ragas, so many musicians singing there.

The praanic wind, water and fire sing; the Righteous Judge of Dharma sings at Your Door. record sing.

Chitr and Gupt, the angels of the conscious and the subconscious who record actions, and the Righteous Judge of Dharma who judges this record sing.

Shiva, Brahma and the Goddess of Beauty, ever adorned, sing.

91

Indra, seated upon His Throne, sings with the deities at Your Door.

The Siddhas in Samaadhi sing; the Saadhus sing in contemplation.

The celibates, the fanatics, the peacefully accepting and the fearless warriors sing.

The Pandits, the religious scholars who recite the Vedas, with the supreme sages of all the ages, sing.

The Mohinis, the enchanting heavenly beauties who entice hearts in this world, in paradise, and in the underworld of the subconscious sing.

ਜਪੁਜੀ ਸਾਹਿਬ

The celestial jewels created by You, and the sixty-eight holy places of pilgrimage sing.

The brave and mighty warriors sing; the spiritual heroes and the four sources of creation sing.

The planets, solar
systems and galaxies,
created and arranged by
Your Hand, sing.

They alone sing, who are
pleasing to Your Will.
Your devotees are
imbued with the Nectar
of Your Essence.

ਜਪੁਜੀ ਸਾਹਿਬ

95

So many others sing, they do not come to mind. O Nanak, how can I consider them all?

That True Lord is True, Forever True, and True is His Name.

He is, and shall always be. He shall not depart, even when this Universe which He has created departs.

ਜਪੁਜੀ ਸਾਹਿਬ

He created the world, with its various colors, species of beings, and the variety of Maya.

Having created the creation, He watches over it Himself, by His Greatness.

He does whatever He pleases. No order can be issued to Him.

He is the King, the King of kings, the Supreme Lord and Master of kings. Nanak remains subject to His Will.

Make contentment your ear-rings, humility your begging bowl, and meditation the ashes you apply to your body.

Let the remembrance of death be the patched coat you wear, let the purity of virginity be your way in the world, and let faith in the Lord be your walking stick.

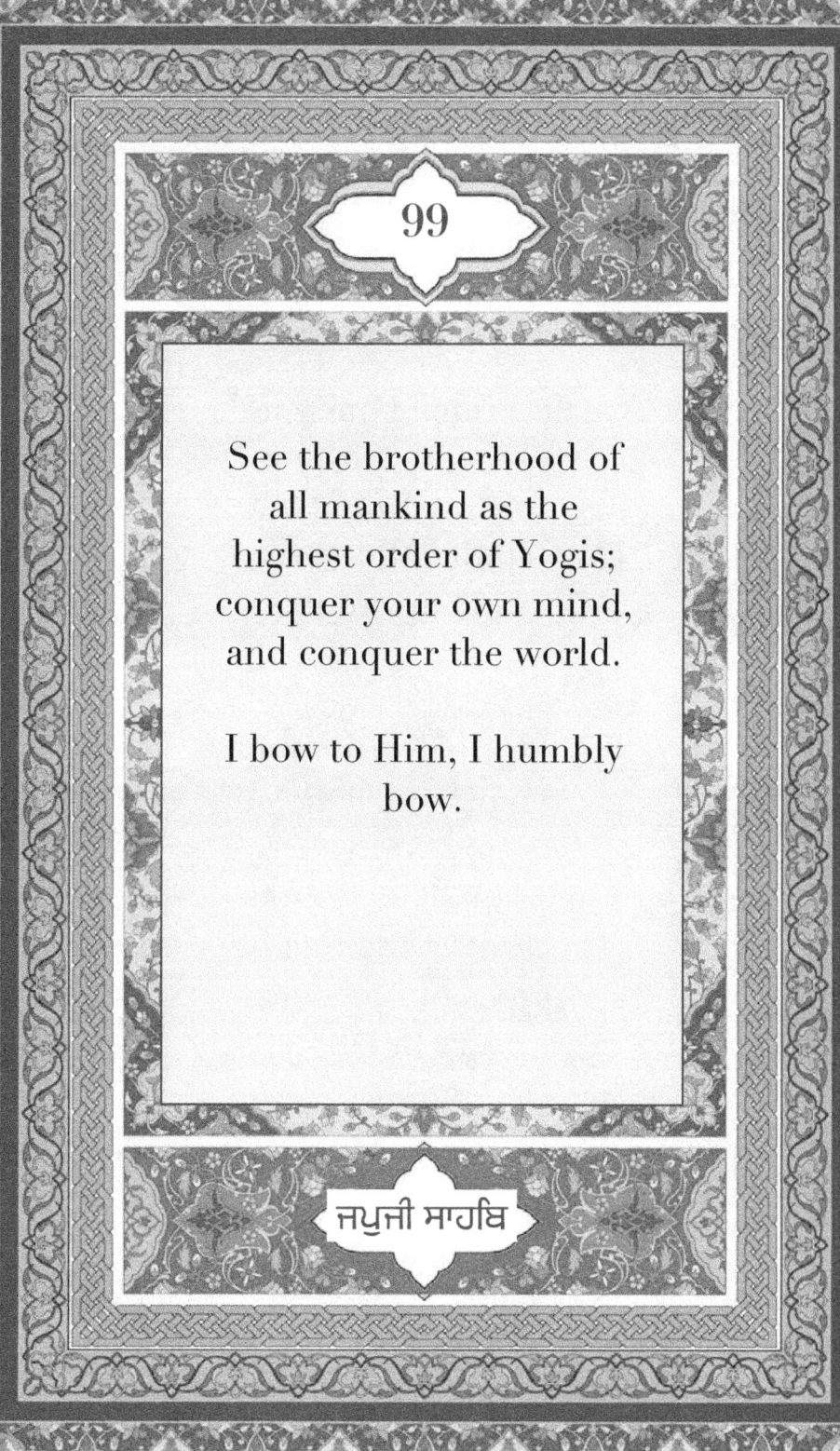

99

See the brotherhood of all mankind as the highest order of Yogis; conquer your own mind, and conquer the world.

I bow to Him, I humbly bow.

ਜਪੁਜੀ ਸਾਹਿਬ

The Primal One, the Pure Light, without beginning, without end. Throughout all the ages, He is One and the Same.

Let spiritual wisdom be your food, and compassion your attendant. The Sound-current of the Naad vibrates in each and every heart.

ਜਪੁਜੀ ਸਾਹਿਬ

101

He Himself is the Supreme Master of all; wealth and miraculous spiritual powers, and all other external tastes and pleasures, are all like beads on a string.

Union with Him, and separation from Him, come by His Will. We come to receive what is written in our destiny.

ਜਪੁਜੀ ਸਾਹਿਬ

I bow to Him,
I humbly bow.

The Primal One, the
Pure Light, without
beginning, without end.
Throughout all the ages,
He is One and the
Same.

ਜਪੁਜੀ ਸਾਹਿਬ

103

The One Divine Mother conceived and gave birth to the three deities.

One, the Creator of the World; One, the Sustainer; and One, the Destroyer.

He makes things happen according to the Pleasure of His Will. Such is His Celestial Order.

ਜਪੁਜੀ ਸਾਹਿਬ

He watches over all, but none see Him. How wonderful this is!

I bow to Him, I humbly bow.

The Primal One, the Pure Light, without beginning, without end. Throughout all the ages, He is One and the Same.

105

On world after world are His Seats of Authority and His Storehouses.

Whatever was put into them, was put there once and for all.

Having created the creation, the Creator Lord watches over it.

ਜਪੁਜੀ ਸਾਹਿਬ

O Nanak, True is the Creation of the True Lord.

I bow to Him, I humbly bow.

The Primal One, the Pure Light, without beginning, without end. Throughout all the ages, He is One and the Same.

ਜਪੁਜੀ ਸਾਹਿਬ

If I had 100,000 tongues, and these were then multiplied twenty times more, with each tongue,

I would repeat, hundreds of thousands of times, the Name of the One, the Lord of the Universe.

Along this path to our Husband Lord, we climb the steps of the ladder, and come to merge with Him.

Hearing of the etheric realms, even worms long to come back home.

O Nanak, by His Grace He is obtained. False are the boastings of the false.

No power to speak, no power to keep silent.

No power to beg, no power to give.

No power to live, no power to die.

No power to rule, with wealth and occult mental powers.

No power to gain intuitive understanding, spiritual wisdom and meditation.

No power to find the way to escape from the world.

He alone has the Power in His Hands. He watches over all.

ਜਪੁਜੀ ਸਾਹਿਬ

O Nanak, no one is high or low.

Nights, days, weeks and seasons; wind, water, fire and the nether regions--in the midst of these, He established the earth as a home for Dharma.

Upon it, He placed the various species of beings.

Their names are uncounted and endless.

By their deeds and their actions, they shall be judged.

God Himself is True, and True is His Court.

ਜਪੁਜੀ ਸਾਹਿਬ

There, in perfect grace and ease, sit the self-elect, the self-realized Saints.

They receive the Mark of Grace from the Merciful Lord.

The ripe and the unripe, the good and the bad, shall there be judged.

ਜਪੁਜੀ ਸਾਹਿਬ

O Nanak, when you go home, you will see this.

This is righteous living in the realm of Dharma.

And now we speak of the realm of spiritual wisdom.

ਜਪੁਜੀ ਸਾਹਿਬ

So many winds, waters and fires; so many Krishnas and Shivas.

So many Brahmas, fashioning forms of great beauty, adorned and dressed in many colors.

So many worlds and lands for working out karma. So very many lessons to be learned!

So many Indras, so many moons and suns, so many worlds and lands. So many Siddhas and Buddhas, so many Yogic masters. So many goddesses of various kinds.

So many demi-gods and demons, so many silent sages. So many oceans of jewels.

So many ways of life, so many languages. So many dynasties of rulers.

So many intuitive people, so many selfless servants. O Nanak, His limit has no limit!

In the realm of wisdom, spiritual wisdom reigns supreme.

ਜਪੁਜੀ ਸਾਹਿਬ

The Sound-current of the Naad vibrates there, amidst the sounds and the sights of bliss.

In the realm of humility,
the Word is Beauty.

Forms of incomparable
beauty are fashioned
there.

These things cannot be
described.

One who tries to speak
of these shall regret the
attempt.

The intuitive consciousness, intellect and understanding of the mind are shaped there. The consciousness of the spiritual warriors and the Siddhas, the beings of spiritual perfection, are shaped there. In the realm of karma, the Word is Power.

ਜਪੁਜੀ ਸਾਹਿਬ

121

No one else dwells there, except the warriors of great power, the spiritual heroes.

They are totally fulfilled, imbued with the Lord's Essence.

Myriads of Sitas are there, cool and calm in their majestic glory.

ਜਪੁਜੀ ਸਾਹਿਬ

Their beauty cannot be described.

Neither death nor deception comes to those, within whose minds the Lord abides.

ਜਪੁਜੀ ਸਾਹਿਬ

The devotees of many worlds dwell there.

They celebrate; their minds are imbued with the True Lord.

In the realm of Truth, the Formless Lord abides.

Having created the creation, He watches over it. By His Glance of Grace, He bestows happiness.

There are planets, solar systems and galaxies.

If one speaks of them, there is no limit, no end.

ਜਪੁਜੀ ਸਾਹਿਬ

125

There are worlds upon worlds of His Creation.

As He commands, so they exist.

He watches over all, and contemplating the creation, He rejoices.

ਜਪੁਜੀ ਸਾਹਿਬ

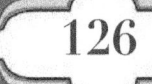

O Nanak, to describe this is as hard as steel!

Let self-control be the furnace, and patience the goldsmith.

Let understanding be the anvil, and spiritual wisdom the tools.

ਜਪੁਜੀ ਸਾਹਿਬ

With the Fear of God as the bellows, fan the flames of tapa, the body's inner heat.

In the crucible of love, melt the Nectar of the Name, and mint the True Coin of the Shabad, the Word of God.

Such is the karma of those upon whom He has cast His Glance of Grace.

O Nanak, the Merciful Lord, by His Grace, uplifts and exalts them.

Air is the Guru, Water is the Father, and Earth is the Great Mother of all.

ਜਪੁਜੀ ਸਾਹਿਬ

Day and night are the two nurses, in whose lap all the world is at play.

Good deeds and bad deeds-the record is read out in the Presence of the Lord of Dharma.

According to their own actions, some are drawn closer, and some are driven farther away.

Those who have meditated on the Naam, the Name of the Lord, and departed after having worked by the sweat of their brows-- O Nanak, their faces are radiant in the Court of the Lord, and many are saved along with them!

ਜਪੁਜੀ ਸਾਹਿਬ

Guru Nanak

ਜਪੁਜੀ ਸਾਹਿਬ